FEATHERED FREAKS

FEATHERED FREAKS

Smith
Street
Books

ntroduction

Birds have always had a hold on our hearts and imaginations.

They symbolize hope, freedom, and, with their miraculous capacity for flight, the promise of limitless possibilities.

They're also absolutely absurd.

This book celebrates our more unique feathered friends, from the gorgeous golden pheasant to the blotchy, balding marabou stork.

As the planet's most diverse land vertebrates, there were always bound to be a few oddballs, and it's these weirdos that make birds so special.

The bizarre shapes, colors, calls, and behaviors are a triumph of biodiversity and reveal how birds have survived and thrived across all habitats. And as the climate crisis pushes more species to extinction, it's a timely reminder to cherish and champion the rare and the unusual.

Whether they make you swoon, make you scared, or make you chuckle, we hope you come away with a newfound appreciation for these flighty freaks.

Hooded Merganser

Lophodytes cucullatus

While other ducks nest some distance away, this North American fish-eater is the only one to nest right next to the water. We assume it's to cut down on the commute and free up more time for that epic haircare routine.

Andean Cock-of-the-rock

Rupicola peruvianus

Someone must have run out of orange paint halfway through making the national bird of Peru. Still, it's a vibe, and at least the slapdash paint job is better than the bird's call, which has been uncharitably described as "a cross between a chainsaw and a squealing pig."

Spotted Eagle-owl

Bubo africanus

It's a shame to see such a stunning set of pins on an animal that prefers flying over strutting down the catwalk. In any case, a varied diet of insects, mammals, birds, amphibians, and reptiles ensures this bird is always runway ready.

Secretary Bird

Sagittarius serpentarius

Joan Holloway step aside, the secretarial pool has a new pecking order. These leggy raptors stride across the savanna grasslands in pairs hunting for prey. Once captured, they stomp on their victims until immobilized!

Rockhopper Penguin

udyptes chrysocome

These cool-climate waddlers (with eyelashes that just won't quit) have an appearance that perfectly matches their personality – they're the certified punks of the penguin family.

King Vulture

Sarcoramphus papa

It takes a special kind of majesty to pull off a bald look – not to mention a bright-orange wattle (that funky, fleshy bit above the beak). These sassy scavangers really must be seen to be believed, and for that you'll have to head to Central or South America.

Muscovy Duck

airina moschata

We could tell you all about how "Muscovy" means "from Moscow," which doesn't make sense for an American duck, but we know you just want to find out about those red things on its face. Fine. They're called "caruncles," they're totally normal, and no, they're not contagious.

Magnificent Frigatebird

Fregata magnificens

To be fair, that large, red, inflatable throat pouch is magnificent, if but extremely strange. Somewhat less magnificent, however, is this seabird's reputation for "kleptoparasitism," which involves pestering other birds until they puke, then gobbling the stuff up.

Gloster Canary

Serinus canaria subsp. *domestica*

With one of the most iconic bowl-cut hairdos to be found in the bird kingdom, these petite, round chirpers are also known for their sing-song whistle. First bred in the 1920s, these gentle feathered freaks have become a fan-favorite with canary lovers worldwide.

Philippine Eagle

Pithecophaga jefferyi

Also known as the monkey-eating eagle (yes, you read that correctly), this shaggy-crested, Filipino raptor has a reputation for munching on some of our closely related primate pals. Best not get too close.

Great Curassow

rax rubra

Cloaked in a glossy, black plumage with a majestic crest, these large, low-lying birds reside in the tropical rainforests of the central Americas. With ancestry that extends back nine million years, these mohawked marvels are sadly now a vulnerable species, with much of their native habitat now destroyed by deforestation.

Common Ostrich

Struthio camelus

Behold the world's largest and heaviest bird! With a long neck, large eyes, and a trunk full of feathers, these colossal Southern African creatures command respect from animal and humans alike. Cited as the most dangerous bird on the planet, they really are freaks of nature.

Great Blue Heron

Ardea herodias

This stately bird – with a neck that just won't quit – is found in the wetlands and open waters of North and Central America. Like Derek Zoolander, this creature doesn't move a lot and nails *the look* everytime.

Great Gray Owl

rix nebulosa

As fluffy and teddybear-like as this owl may appear, its sharp beak can make easy work of nearby rodents – including squirrels, hares, and even ducks.

Tufted Puffin

Fratercula cirrhata

It isn't balding, thank you very much, and the yellow feathers on its head aren't a desperate combover. Instead, we say it's "tufted." This definitely-not-balding bird is the largest of the marine birds known as puffins – another polite word, from "puff," meaning "swollen."

Toco Toucan

Ramphastos toco

Despite its long-time collaboration with Guinness, you won't find the toco toucan anywhere near Ireland. Rather, this orange-beaked freak flaps about South America (as well as on the side of Froot Loops cereal boxes).

Vulturine Guineafowl

ryllium vulturinum

This cobalt-blue beauty derives its name from its vulture-like bald head. Unlike its namesake, however, this bird is not for flying long stretches. The guineafowl is a better runner, spending its days darting across the African savanna.

Tawny Frogmouth

Podargus strigoides

These nocturnal hunters – one of Australia's finest forms of pest control – have mastered the art of camouflage in their branch-hued plumage. Like their owl siblings, the frogmouth is most active at night.

Southern Cassowary

Casuarius casuarius

Commonly referred to as a "living dinosaur," this six-foot tall, 170-pound beast lets off a terrifying, deep growl that we like to think would have sent the velociraptors running

Lettered Aracari

Pteroglossus inscriptus

This tiny toucan gets its name from the squiggly, little markings on its bill. Perching in the upper-Amazon basin, these peckers live the high life, taking over abandoned woodpecker nests for their real-estate of choice.

Spinifex Pigeon

Geophaps plumifera

This pint-sized, outback pigeon with punk-rock plumage spends its time in the expanses of arid and semi-arid Australia. The spinifex pigeon's diet of choice ... spinifex.

Golden Pheasant

Chrysolophus pictus

Also aptly known as the rainbow pheasant, these swanky brightly hued gamebirds are native to the mountains of western China, where they spend their time trawling the forest floors for grains, leaves, and insects.

Victoria Crowned Pigeon

ura victoria

Like an upcoming socialite from the pages of *Tatler*, this pigeon (a more urbane version of its gray city cousins) wears its own conspicuous fascinator and saunters the streets to encourage admiration from all passers-by.

Eurasian Hoopoe

Upupa epops

This cinnamon-colored beauty boasts a tall, dotted crest
and zebra striped wings that are completely unique in the
avian kingdom. Legend has it that its haunting "hoop-
oop-oop" song is believed to foreshadow death.

Eastern Pink Cockatoo

Cacatua leadbeateri

One of these Australian outback darlings took home the Guinness World Record for the oldest parrot, living to the ripe age of 82. Despite the bird's reputation for lifelong monogamy, that particular old codger, named Cookie, rejected his female mate because "she wasn't nice to him."

Polish Bantam Chicken

Gallus gallus domesticus

There are a few key differences between this chicken and your grandmother, despite the same short, tight perm. For example, while Nana may be doting, the Polish isn't fussed about its chicks, and doesn't even bother sitting on its eggs ... although we hope that last bit is also true for Granny.

Crested Partridge

Rollulus rouloul

With all due respect to Latin speakers, you can't help but wonder whether they were just making it up when they gave this roly-poly bird the scientific name *Rollulus rouloul*. Understandably, they waddle about more than they fly, and forage for food on the ground – or, in Latin, the *Groundulus groundground*.

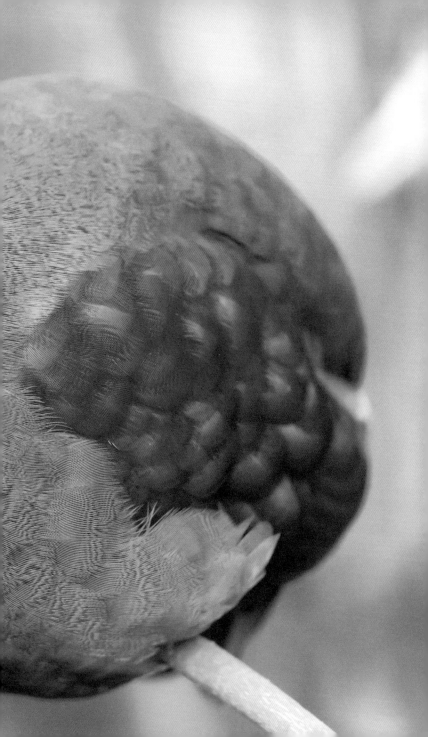

Shoebill

Balaeniceps rex

Nope. Absolutely not. Hard pass. Nothing we say about this stork-like nightmare is going to make you feel any less terrified. Like the fact that it eats crocodiles. Or a mention of the machine-gun rattle as it clatters its razor sharp bill. Best just move right along.

Ornate Hawk-eagle

izaetus ornatus

This grumpy guts may seem more "ornery" than "ornate," but don't say that to its face – this skilled raptor can capture prey twice its weight. The "ornate" refers in part to the crest of black feathers it raises when excited, which, although hard to imagine here, does sometimes happen.

Sword-billed Hummingbird

Ensifera ensifera

This tiny speed-flapper is the only bird to boast a bill
longer than its body. Its mighty sword means it has uniq
claim over the precious nectars of certain passionflower
In fact, its bill is so long that its body is permanently
tipped upward to avoid face-planting and it has to use
its tiny feet to preen.

Blue-footed Booby

Sula nebouxii

Before there were Crocs, these fashion pioneers invented ugly footwear, with a blue hue courtesy of nutrients from the fish they eat. And like Crocs, their kicks are, regrettabl both waterproof and practical, playing a role in the seabir mating rituals and helping keep their young warm.

Bali Myna

...copsar rothschildi

Bali's blue-eyed official faunal emblem very sensibly dines on insects, fruit, worms, and small reptiles, because it would be asking for trouble to eat spaghetti bolognese in such a snow-white coat.

Dalmatian Pelican

Pelecanus crispus

To "give someone the dirty bird" usually means to flip someone off, but it could also literally refer to gifting this disheveled unit. With a wing span the length of a family hatchback, this largest of the pelican species might be a little trickier to deliver.

Wood Duck

Aix sponsa

The "wood" is a nod to the fact that this is one of only a few waterfowl to hang about in trees, while the scientific name translates to "bridal duck," for its dapper, wedding-ready appearance. Judging by the power clashing, it must be more of a smart casual ceremony.

Spectacled Eider

omateria fischeri

Like a geek-chic set of thick-rimmed specs with the lenses popped out, the "goggles" on this high arctic diving duck are purely for show. Its eyesight clearly needs no correction, as it can hunt out clams and other small, hard-to-spot snacks up to 250 feet underwater.

Rufous Hornbill

Buceros hydrocorax

IKEA could only dream of a bird that comes with built-in shelving space, or a "casque." But wait, there's more: It also tells the time! Sometimes called "the clock of the mountains," this Filipino timekeeper lets out periodical nasal honks, which can be heard from a mile away.

Barred Eagle-owl

Ketupa sumatrana

At a glance, this owl may look like it has its eyelash extension game on point, but they're not lashes. These "ear tufts" are said to help them blend into their surroundings, which would make sense if their surroundings were beauty salons, not the forests of Asia

American White Pelican

lecanus erythrorhynchos   It may not appear graceful here, but this pelican – one of North America's largest birds – is quite a sight in flight. Arguably even more impressive, at least as a party trick, is its ability to chug up to three gallons in one gulp.

Wild Turkey

Meleagris gallopavo

Equal parts beloved and maligned, this American icon and Thanksgiving symbol may not be the most good-looking specimen, but it sure is good at looking – with eyesight three times sharper than 20/20 vision.

Paradise Riflebird

Ptiloris paradisea

This Australian bird-of-paradise's courtship display involves more than just pressing its wingtips together and shouting, "Look at me!" It spends years rehearsing a elaborate dance, which involves hopping, rocking side to side, and even a variation of dabbing.

Snowy Owl

bo scandiacus

North America's heaviest owl gets its heft from a bounty
of thick white feathers that keep it warm and insulated
on the icy tundras – or at least that's what it says.

American Flamingo

Phoenicopterus ruber

These bombshells are actually born a humdrum gray, and only get their vivid pink from pigments in their food. As for why they prefer to stand on one leg, there's a simple explanation: If they lifted the other leg, they'd fall over.

Kagu

Rhynochetos jubatus

This elegant strutter is known in its New Caledonia home as "the ghost of the forest," for its almost spectral gray appearance. Despite sporting a remarkable set of wings, it would rather not waste them on something as uncouth as flying, saving them instead for impressing mates.

Hoatzin

Opisthocomus hoazin

Yes, it looks like they rolled straight out of the nest this morning. Thing is, these striking South American birds smell like it too. Often referred to as the "stinkbird," they ferment food in their stomachs, similar to a cow, giving them a pong reminiscent of manure.

Yellow-billed Hornbill

Tockus leucomelas

A curved yellow bill won this African bird the apt nickname "the flying banana." Like many birds in hot areas, instead of sweating, it dissipates heat with that beak. So, literally: cool bananas.

Malay Crested Fireback

Lophura rufa

Don't let the mask and the tufted hat fool you: This pheasant is endemic to the lowland forests of the Thai-Malay Peninsula and Sumatra, and didn't just get lost on the way to a fancy masquerade ball.

Common Potoo

yctibius griseus

While the feathers do wonders for camouflaging among branches, that moody expression sticks out like a sore thumb. Not helping this nocturnal negative Nancy's case is its song, which has been described as sounding exactly like the words "poor me, all alone."

Blue-and-yellow Macaw

Ara ararauna

As if the astonishing splashes of blue and yellow weren't already turning heads, these chatty, outgoing parrots often scream to get attention. That's not to say they're completely shameless divas, as they have been observed to blush when interacting with humans.

Rufous Hummingbird

Selasphorus rufus

This pocket-sized dynamo is not mucking about. Despite clocking in at a little over three inches long, it constantly picks fights with other birds, including the much larger blue jay, and braves a migratory path equivalent to almost 80 million times the length of its wee body.

Silvery-cheeked Hornbill

ycanistes brevis

Like a credit card statement with duplicate transactions, this African bird appears to have been double-billed. However, that extra bill is actually a hollow "horn" that amplifies the volume of its honking calls.

Gray Crowned Crane

Balearica regulorum

You don't just get a crown like that; you have to earn it. This national bird of Uganda deserves its royal adornment. It was the very first crane on the scene, beating out the others by tens of millions of years, and remains the only one that builds its nest – or throne – in trees.

Water Thick-knee

Burhinus vermiculatus

Oh come on, they're not that thick. Okay, maybe they're a little bit knobbly. Thick knees or not, this small African stoned curlew has big cojones, building its nests next to crocodiles and chasing them away from *their* turf.

Marabou Stork

ptoptilos crumenifer

If storks really did deliver babies, you'd be forgiven for requesting a different courier. These bald scavengers feast on carrion and human garbage, and, like the babies they thankfully don't deliver, sometimes poop all over themselves, which helps keep them cool in the African heat.

White-cheeked Turaco

Menelikornis leucotis

The "white-cheeked" in the name, while accurate, is really burying the lede here. These members of the Musophagidae family – literally "banana eaters" – are the only birds that are truly green and red – all the others are just tricks of light and reflection.

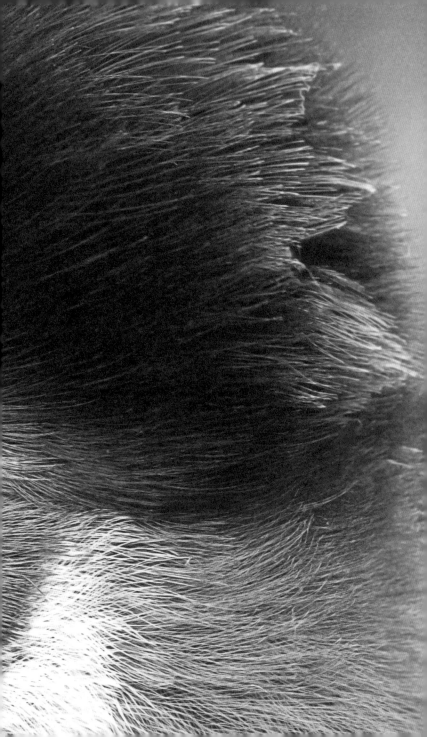

Published in 2024 by Smith Street Books
Naarm (Melbourne) | Australia
smithstreetbooks.com

ISBN: 978-1-9230-4948-2

Smith Street Books respectfully acknowledges the Wurundjeri People of the Kulin Nation, who are the Traditional Owners of the land on which we work, and we pay our respects to their Elders past and present.

Publisher: Paul McNally
Designer: Andy Warren
Text: Tobias Fehily
Editor: Lucy Grant
Printed & bound in China by C&C Offset Printing Co., Ltd.

Book 335
10 9 8 7 6 5 4 3 2 1